Rock Worn By Water

Florence Chard Dacey

D1455498

Plain View Press
P. O. 42255
Austin, TX 78704

plainviewpress.net
sb@plainviewpress.net
1-512-441-2452

Copyright Florence Dacey 2009. All rights reserved.
ISBN: 978-0-911051-21-6
Library of Congress Number: 2009920264

Cover art *Minnehaha Falls 2* by Elizabeth Erickson

Acknowledgments

Thanks to Elizabeth Erickson for her unflagging interest in my life as a poet, Pat Kaluza for editing assistance, Nancy Paddock for her help with revising an earlier version of this manuscript, Sandy Spieler and In the Heart of the Beast Puppet and Mask Theater for steady inspiration, my family and friends for their encouragement and love. I am grateful to Susan Bright and Plain View Press for helping to bring this work to the world.

My appreciation also goes to the Southwest Minnesota Arts and Humanities Council, the New York Mills Cultural Center, the McKnight Foundation, and Norcroft, for providing time to work on poems in this book.

Acknowledgements are made to the following publications and websites in which these poems or earlier versions of them appeared: "Down the Hill" in *Nimrod*; "The Grandmothers" and "Certificate of Need" in *Albatross*; "The Collar" in *Dust and Fire*; "In Autumn" in *Avocet*; "What I Did Not See," "Trees I have Known," and "Lightest of Rains" in *101 Names for the Beloved*; "Threshold" in *To Sing Along the Way: Minnesota Women Poets from Pre-Territorial Days to the Present*; "During War Times" and "Disappear" in *Farming Words*; "Prairie Weather" in *County Lines*; "When We Forget the Water" in *In the Heart Of the Beast May Day Tabloid* and as part of Sandy Spieler's *Water Shrine*; "With the Whales" appearing online on the Minnesota Artists website mnartists.org as part of their Five Minutes of Fame contest; "After All of My Life" winner of What Light Contest, appearing online on mnartists.org and magersandquinn.com (Magers and Quinn Bookstore, Minneapolis); "Waves," "Cottonwood," and "Upland Sandpiper" appearing online on morning earth.org.

Dedicated to
the waters
rocks
trees
sky
and wild creatures
of this only world of ours
and to all who work
to protect the planet.

In memory of
my parents
Pauline and Warren Chard
who taught me to
love the earth.

Contents

What Language Is This?

Make Everything Move

Her Small Old Ear Still Open

Whatever You Do

What Language Is This?

Invitation

All day the wind tries to seduce me,
her face all gentle creases,
her supple voice full
of compliments I credit.

> *Come away!*
> *You can still tap-dance down this hill.*

The wind hides coyly in the oak
till I shake her with my bold fantasy.
I have young breezes in my old blood.

She can't resist,
ancient wind
whirling in her white
stripped way, falling down
and getting up and holding
out her whistling hands.

Colors on the Hill

What language is this swath of chartreuse,
aisle of crimson, purple, orange fires?

Greens advance too, like soft armies of muted spears.
A single maple flashes there like a fresh wound.

Are we in a church? an old man asks. The sun blesses
his pale face and the white of a spectral birch far up on a hill.

This is the most beautiful thing I've even seen,
a woman tells her young girls, held in the wind.

I want to take each one's hand and swim out
past the mountain of color, like a single, red leaf.

So Like the Trees

A maple breaks off close to the ground,
goes down with a sudden crack in the northwest wind.

Even young ones can snap in the middle
and flop over, ragged and torn, welcoming rot.

Others die from a flaw deep inside.
Their leaves wither and cling

while some keep their broad, tall trunks to the end.
Bark slowly stripped,

one limb then another slips down
till only smooth pale skin

lingers in dark woods,
claiming the moon's eerie light

in that hollow within
for sun and rain.

Quiet Day in the North Woods

Tamaracks have lit all their cathedrals—

    this gold sears deep in human veins.

Maple leaves hammer the video of the mind—

    lichen muffles echoes of alarm.

Silence mimics your mangled plan—

    the loon laughs into cold memory.

Jammed in the synapses, the quiet takes out the grid of your

    lonely voice, bringing down the fortress.

Cottonwood

Fountain of moonlight,
spry upstart among the sprawling
cedars, the flushed wind sends
you swaying into fall.

Like tears
your fluttering heart-
shaped leaves turn gold.

Inside you pour
tunnels of rough stars.

You want to climb up to the lowering sky,
pull your feet from out this dry hillside.

We see your sisters along the river
throwing light off
as young girls do water after
dips or a naked dash in rain,
growing fast and soft
to break,
to die that much sooner.

In Autumn

I want to rub rose and carmine pulled
from maple limbs deep into my palms.

Paint my solitude lemon-amber,
watch the spectrum widen.

Press carnelian leaves
against my frown.

Swallow this crimson and cream
till my insides cure.

Stride into honey-yellow trees,
waft forth, breathe whole again.

I want silver-pink rhythm of bark
to jostle my distortions,

grizzled wanton taproot
to pierce the fetid past,

brazen stem, fork of
lightning to incite,

before the winds disperse me.

Prairie Weather

Winter storms are fierce, pulling us away from meager mind.
Snow catapults under our doors and corrals cars into single lanes.
Wind sprouts white talons.
It throws up partitions between us and the landmarks we live by.
Blizzards pull us down into fitful isolation.
We peer befuddled out of small islands
breathed onto frosty windowpanes.
When it clears a bit, we hurry to town for bread and milk.

In early summer the air grows heavy
and pulses like an artery ready to burst.
Ahead of one tornado, tufted layers of grey cloud scout silently,
going too fast and packed to the limit.
The twister roars over that hill, down into the river valley.
One old man dies, under his pickup.
Broken-off trees by the road keep
the history fresh in our album of fears.

In between, rare floods sometimes accompany spring blizzards.
Old and young fill sandbags together. The talk is easy, the topic set.
The river has its way a while, gives misery a muddy suit,
takes back some land we thought we owned.

When the great storms begin, I stand in my backyard prairie circle.
I gauge and, if I must, call for some mercy.
But usually I call in silence and inward exhilaration for the storm.
In guilt and horror at human folly,
in rage and in wonder at all our power,
I call and call, to be confounded by such weather.

Upland Sandpiper

Sitting on the earth, studying
      prairie smoke, its soft purple plumed
            tresses grasped between my fingers,

I noticed she'd come up
      from the reclaimed ditch, her wide-eyed look
            like a child's, startled from her dream.

Her body gleamed like a woods
      mottled and laced, with barred browns and whites
            and sighs of wind under feather.

I wanted to hear her mournful whistle.
      I wanted to defend her pinkish buff eggs.
            Did she carry deep in that delicate brain

perched on her long neck
      the memory of harm from my kind?
            Was my face a known alarm?

She looked at me straight on
      making her head a slim demarcation. Her neck
            pressed forward, back, forward, back

until I too had to move,
      bringing us both to that moment when
            the wild one understands,
                flees.

Prairie Smoke

Everywhere, everywhere,
like the endless embrace
of young lovers,
the prairie smoke
let their drooping lavender buds
swell and spill clouds
threaded with amethyst
yet softer
than a child's first hair.
From each root
the command is to dance.
Dance as you sit
and pretend you are still ten,
too beautiful and light
to stay on this earth,
yet wildly happy here
with your kind—
the ones who let their hair
be taken by wind,
who throw their arms
around each other,
around you,
the violet spun cloak of your life,
the fragile, brief riot of you.

What I Did Not See

A bee complained how I kept him from his cup of purple flower
so I moved.

A larva painted like the badlands crawled through the hole
in my straw hat, free to escape to villas in the prairie grass.

I found the innards of a deer, the matted fur, hoof and bone
arranged as for a painter's eye.

Most things hid from me, a quiet perpendicular
piercing the sparrow's horizon.

But I knew they were there—
the fists and elbows of jostling seeds,
lilting eggs of the chirping sparrow,
ants with their long, serious paths
and somewhere a snake, a vole
well apprised of one another.

What I did not see steadies me, miles from prairie now,
as a rock, as my father's unsaid words.

I know a hill where prairie smoke will write
its pink and purple story every June, even as
machines not far away break the earth to make another road.

I know each time I must, I can come home
to prairie wide with light and all those hidden there
who never raise a gun or promise love
or ask of me what I cannot give.

Maynard in the Perfect Corn

Corn is high and near perfect this July
along Maynard's road, our walk.
He enters one dark narrow tunnel
and is lost to me.

Maynard hasn't read of Terminator seeds
genetically engineered,
of the killing of the soil
and our family farms.
He's a dog, won't wonder
if these glossy leaves
and plush, tasseled ears
are part of that misguided scheme.

He'll wander
in that lush, shady forest.
He'll smell the earth,
roots, fallen kernels.
Heady, he'll emerge
with corn pollen
on his broad back,
pale twists of life
on the black ground
of his body.

He'll carry them
unthinking
and shake them off
in his own good time,
the perfect pollen
from the perfect corn.

Field of Rye

That July day we came to visit the farm,
the field of rye lay softer than rain,
a swath of bowed glory too radiant to touch.

But we were invited to pull on a stalk
and free a small, hard seed. A child
held her seed, ran and plunged like a comet

into a great drift of straw, resurrected into
a world of peace where a man stood
with hands exploding only

from brown and yellow seeds
alive with sun and water,
the hidden lives of the land he tends.

As if the good harvest could not end.
As if we had only to say *yes*
and our hands would be filled.

Make Everything Move

Waterfall

High up the waterfall begins
at the icy jeweled tips of spruces,
the suicides' captured eyes,
in the spider webs holding
mountains secure under one moon,
within the volcanic craters
where the anchors of stone are rising.

High, high up in the mother's songs
it masses, weaving itself
out of bedrock, seed and cloud.

The waterfall meets us
like a fleet of ghostly galleons
under a halcyon sun,
intrigues like the race
of pink roses with death,
overcomes us.

We are invited to leap now,
to plummet and scatter
and assail the heavens with cries,
history taut in our arms,
parents and babies and lovers
in our broody arms,
ourselves in our arms
turned to gorgeous true words
pliant ribbons spun by god—

who we were,
who we have become.

Down the Hill

You can start by the Upper Sioux Agency
where the cedar and sage still wait.
You can start by becoming an eight-year-old child
in terror at indiscriminate death.
Or start as a river-man, practical, sad.
Start where you are trying to live with birds
somehow, as a woman.

Tonight this woman, wearing all the colors,
comes down the hill with a loyal dog
who ranges and leaps in snowdrifts, circles back
to her halting, archaic steps. She carries
nothing with her but that terror,
though she has sensed the bones of the red ones,
the white ones, under this snow,
knows she walks always over the bodies of children.

She has tried being deaf and blind, silent and true.
Nothing saves you from the path down, awkward, always
off-balance, down by full moon and stars,
the very same stars to remind you,
through the careless arc of the night, the stately
sumac, crying to the earth through your rough
boots, pausing to let the oaks breathe you
in, release you to nothing again.

We are making this valley as we go,
brushing the earth from our eyes.
The old ice shatters in us.
We rush away from ourselves.
Flickering souls hang dense in these trees.
Twelve eagles leave the mounded grief at last,
circle, begin to feed in our opened waters.

The Grandmothers

Read into the record at a public information meeting
on the burning of PCBs at a power plant in
Granite Falls, Minnesota

When I think of this ancient river valley,
I think of the grandmothers,
women like *Woman Who Talks to Iron*
and the other native women, their bodies arched
like prairie grasses over a shining river,
their hands cupping water for a child
who will never imagine he is a rusted machine.

I think of the white grandmothers,
water in their kettles
and fish no one was afraid to eat.

Now, in these waters of March,
in these ghostly fogs rising along the valley,
I think of the grandmothers' spirits
shaped like rock worn by water.

I think the grandmothers in their grief and grace
have come up from the river into this place
and they are carrying in their whole bodies
a dying river
and they would like to speak
to the ones who have sold their hearts.

Near Pine Lake

That summer dusk
I stopped to hear the frogs
alongside the road, in a little bog.

One frog's voice burst up
from lush reeds
with pure authority.

Another, higher pitched,
over in that far clump,
affirmed this was their kingdom.

Back and forth—how many I don't know—
they boasted unabashed and boisterously
of their mere being, to water and muck, the darkening marsh.

I looked at this small wilderness
where they lurked like dragons,
like temples of dark water,

their cloudy eyes and cool blood
alive in their cadence
of this birthing and ending place.

I thought of the water we sicken
and the swamps we drain, the years we take
to carefully determine something might be amiss

while the young boys capture
frogs without eyes,
frogs with too many eyes.

With the Whales

1.

For a moment we spoke the language
of shark tooth and ocean current
engraved on acres of grey skin,
made our bones vast,
bore barnacle stars on our backs.

Then the whale advanced even closer,
opening her benign eye one long second
to our orange-suited selves
propping up our teary cheeks.

For one life fall, we imagined
our arms banked with cedar
thrown across her homing,
offered for thanks, for forgiveness
as she dove under the little boat,
carefully threaded her universe back and forth,
pushing out everything that passed through her.

Surely we lifted then
the weight of ourselves into
brief spinning joy with her.
Surely we broke from
our cold, bottomless lives,
our measure finally taken.

Continued

2.

After the whale
everything is large and knows
the tiny ancient stars of itself
rising out of the ordinary to spin
its great matter in play, in sheer
spurning of fear.

After the whale
we approach the world as if the past
had fallen away, spewed out
like the gray leviathan's pungent waste.

At your peril
you shall love.
At your peril
you shall not love
these lost bunglers,
these noisy fools
riding the waves
in search of you.

3.

Afterwards, a woman wrote
her call to the whales
who she imaged long years
flaring in the Pacific currents.
She saw they moved according to
their own songs, along melodic, majestic
tremors that intersected her dreams,
the skies she surveyed from jets
and the little tragedies of life on land.

Her call went like this:
Come to me, gray-splotched and scarred beings.
Come with your great unfettered heads
like mountains unchained and your sprouting
and spewing of huge swallows
we take to keep ourselves afloat.
Turn on the blank horizon, our poison forgotten.
Turn on the sun and stars that lead
you past our feeble ports. Bring to us
this innocence, this eye so close, not touching,
this play for no reason, the arc of your wet hurl
turning us, turning to see
we did not kill, we could not kill
what we did not understand.

The Waves

You notice the waves are never still.

The waves change just as your hands do, as needed, as a task arises.

Today, in this world we have made,
all the waves must carry us, keep us from drowning in ourselves
even as they bring us back to ourselves, without illusions.

We're going to scatter, we're going to evaporate.
We're going to not continue as we are, as we imagine we are.

Do you think waves imagine anything?
No, but they haven't needed to
so far.

But now that we are killing water, perhaps they do?
Perhaps they have dreams of a world without us,
without nets and poison and calculator brains.

How much do you love the waves?
Would you say, it would be fine if they washed us
all away, this moment?
Would you drop everything to work to clean the waters?

But here is something we could actually do.
Lie down by the sea
or river or lake or stream
until the water in us
begins a small conversation
with the waves
who are waiting.

Part of Us

Water knows so much by sheer proximity—
the inside of arteries,
the glow of creatures in her depths.

Mostly water as we are,
oughtn't we to guess
how water comprehends?

When the water rises and wrecks
our pitiful refuge, when water mocks
our dams, levees and flood control,

part of us breaks loose and leaps,
an old part that goes everywhere,
touches everything inside and out—

places with no light,
places where we invent
the light we need.

After All of My Life

Such a symphony of wind in trees
and boom of waves, this morning after
thunder, rain. I want to climb
the unfurling birch tree and leap, without thinking.
I want to curl into the cobalt barrel
of the wave and release against these shores.

Such a talking to my face, the truth
of what it means to live here, die here
in each other's company.
Make everything move, make
this old heart and mind shake
this morning after all of my life
I've moved through like a mole,
like a wild turkey lost on the highway.

This is the magic world I never meant to leave.
The lichen are my first sturdy friends and they are many.
Graceful sticks rest across delicate blue flowers
and the dried black flies flutter somehow gaily too, in the web.

My body is a simpler heaviness
on the fire of ancient rock.
My spirit trembles like hidden seeds.
And in the high torn cloud
a dark ring erases itself.

Preparation

Here is what I'll gather up
      for the long winter to come:

The green-blue hours
      water wraps itself around,

the lake lapping a spiral
      of golden poplar leaves
            flung down for luck,

the way what sun made shine
      below the surface seems
          to be shining
               everywhere.

Sail

For my brother, Philip Sutton Chard

Let us board everyone—
the dead ones, a deaf brother,
each of the old lovers
and prancing children
looking sometimes askance.
It's a small boat, a large craft
that holds all, to the tune of Mozart's requiem,
Odetta and U-2, to the turning of Irish reels,
fights and finest soliloquies, to silence.

Every stitch was fine, every rigged word, crucial,
the rudder requested and paid for.

So, board everything, everyone.

You crew. I'll be ballast. I'll perch
in the stern and we'll race.
We'll be, these few hours, all grace,
dipping and rising, leaning and tacking.

Let's imagine the sails never split, the mast never rots.
Let's wrap rope that never burns, never breaks.
Let's see each other as does this vessel
that speeds us toward some mark.
Which and at how many degrees?

And don't you love it,
with the fine sailor rising
to brace the mast
so we catch a dying wind,
go swifter,
win.

Saving Ourselves

Travel to water. Touch
those glittering hands
that sculpt rock to soft torso.

Visit cascading river
sunk in the grave it digs
with roaring fingers.

Rest by small warm pools
set like jewels in rock
where birds can feast on

tiny floating seeds
who cradle their deaths
in rapturous calm.

Lullaby

Water, dream you are a trunk full of blue buttons sprung
from the cloak of night or my grandmother's worn coat.
The scratches on your top are shy birds
skimming the surface like small hopes.

Dream you are an old wooden chair
in the corner of a dusty room.
You believe in arrivals.
Let us lean into you, that familiar lap.

Water, be sunshine.
On wedding days, turn faces wet
with some lost brightness,
a lamp brought into the tent of innocence.

All over the world, come and go
like a deep meaning, yet get nowhere.
Like a forgotten witness,
stay and stay.

Water, dream you are winking like a star.
Only you get the joke.
But be serious too.
Catch stray men in your cloak.

Be the birth cord that anchors
the body and soul of sadness,
the hidden breasts of the mother,
a voice of many weathers.

Water, touch everything.

Clear

When I swim
I lower myself
to where everything
glides unscathed,
grace without pain.

Legs bend
supple as willow.
Paddling arms
arc slow
as manatees.

My spine finds
perfect balance
for head,
heart,
and womb,
ceasing their old quarrel.

I splash and kick
back and forth
to my allotment
of human breaths.

My bones drift
light as birch vessels.

I splay flat
as a bright starfish
carried on tide's decree.

Continued

My ruined hips,
my stiff neck
dissolve
into what we call
water,
really
sheer easing,
the yielding.

Dissolving

Put on a green coat.
Step out with the fawn into the shadows of June maples.
Recline in extravagant grass newly sprung in the forest breaks.
Feel surge of lime, olive, jade, the thornless.

Slip on a rare blue coat and launch tears onto one lake.
Linked dragonfly lovers alight.
Distant loon haunts reveries with his ageless formality.
All murmuring, solace nudges the shore—*Make room, give way.*

Wrap yourself in the red coat that fires fed in the green trees
to make their bark ridge and buckle, lava
spread on water to turn dead souls to ripples.

The scarlet bird out of a dream tells how to take off
coats our mother made, be just children,
colors all leaching, dappled hands dissolving
in light rain, tree, bird, swampy lake.

When We Forget the Water

When we forget the water,
we forget the child
who begins in the water.

When we forget the child,
we forget ourselves

and then
we forget the world.

Her Small Old Ear Still Open

All She Knew

A girl-child pondered:
What is this world?
Named it: *Home.*

What we seem to destroy.
What calls us back from destruction.

Her eyes flashed mutable.
Her mind ranged farther than missiles.

Her hands grew large with words
more obdurate than obelisks.

She kept dreaming
for the dead children,
lost species, raped rivers
her mothers mourned.

She made her own mystery.
Water gave her curve of might.
Ancient trees steadied her.

She learned to love this world here,
persuaded her body
with delicate flowers
and lived so flagrantly
all she knew and didn't.

Retrieval of the Archives

Where have you misplaced
the primer of you, reader once of the great oaks?

What's become of your translations of the sun,
those etymological studies on wonders of the grass?

Can you find where you filed your skin's declaratives on rain,
those drafts of morning glory's blue
and long poetic lines you stole from the willow?

And wherever have you piled
the rough notes that hinged you to stars,
to night and dawn in a child's eyes?

When will you begin your natural autobiography
for wren's amusement, the silent edification of that wind
on which some claim your name first was written?

Cedar (small song)

Oh cedar,
you are cut down now,
gone like the buffalo.

Where is your green?

Where will the deer sleep now?

Who will hide me from the rain?

Oh cedar,
you are cut down now.

Gone is your scent,
gone the blue berries.

In your stump—
Red.

Collar

Smarter than us, the wolf packs
learn to chew off the telemetric collars
scientists place to track them with radio waves.
One pack even teaches another how to do it
using teeth and jaw, the oldest wild defense.

Each wolf knows the collar as a hand
that wants to point her towards a certain thing
that is not a shadowed forest.
She can teach us to take whatever teeth of the soul
we have left and tear away whatever was made
to track us, turn our paths to numbers,
to compromise us without consent, to save us.
Teach us to miss the pack, the jostling
and curving into each other in the cold.

Though we have lost, almost, the smell
of tree's damp descent to forest floor
and taste of unexpected bounty,
the juice of it all,
though our hands and feet rest dainty, fine
and rarely touch the layers
of needle, lichen, stick and scat,
she can teach us that waiting is what our animal does
crossing wilderness in our sleep,
in our soiled pristine beds,
her small old ear still open.

Shadows

What is the vessel for the song of the last jay,
the final scarlet tanager, for their colors stolen from sky and sun?

Where is the bowl deep enough to hold the careless lap
against a pebbled beach of the last pure lake?

Seed of the bristle-coned pine, silvery minnow,
will they lodge one day only in the mind's crumbling vault?

Will the child see only something crimson in our eye,
hear just a muffled song from out our sleeping throat?

Will she have to ride fast away
on nothing but the darting shadows?

The Threshold

The whooping crane is an endangered species, brought back
from near extinction by ingenious humans, but still in peril.

Over our subtle states of mind,
   the fine print,
the whooping crane
   hesitates,
   one foot
poised.

   A single crane
harbors
   vast isolate valleys
under her wings,
   rises like a rarified rig
from managed marshes
   where blue crabs so far still feed
her royal mauve
   feathers ruffling like
white sepulchers in fog.

   And the prow,
the curve of that neck
   graced by wind's egress,
lap of water on shell and egg,
   that head we calculate in
     our paltry arithmetic:

   Fifty nesting pairs
would be
   enough, they say,
sufficient beaks and bones

stern eyes and
feathers enough,
        to fly,
to bear us
        over
                the threshold.

Things Recalled in Sadness and All the Joy Possible

The deep-sea scientist stroking the cuttlefish,
who has a thousand patterns,
who watches the man and is learning a new one.

The Colorado River
wearing away the Glen Canyon Dam
even as its water lights each neon sign in Vegas.

The mere three hundred years
required to restore a tall grass prairie,
persuading the earth of our change of heart.

With two out of three species worldwide
thought to be in decline, the likelihood
ours will eventually join the trend.

Old Tree

Remembering *Prometheus*, cut down in 1964

The scientist went looking for the oldest pine trees.
After five minutes he found one that looked pretty old.
But he couldn't get a good core sample, for some reason.
So he neatly cut it down.

The tree didn't make any sounds when they cut it down
and the scientist didn't see the centuries wafting
up like smoke, all the colors, cries, the daily weather.

He got to the rings right away and started counting.
Counting away, he came up with 4900 years this old tree had lived.
He laughs an embarrassed laugh as he tells of that moment
when he realized he'd cut down the oldest tree yet.

These ancient trees can put out a cone and you can
take the cone and bury the seeds and up rise comely offspring,
which is more than we can always say of our propagation.

A slice of that tree is behind glass in a Las Vegas casino,
just watching, not growing anymore, not taking life
into it and making it part of a living thing, anymore.

Wow, some gambler says, looking at it, his eyes
that hold the universe opening a little wider,
the whorls on his fingertips deepening, just a little.

Stone

Eighty fawns are dead
from what they spray to kill the spider mites
on soybeans this lank summer.
That is, just the carcasses they came across.

Inside my dream that night,
a man sounded a conch, woke me,
said, it is wrong, what he ate,
the flesh of the earth.

Out of the dream I ask:

> *Do we believe in penance?*
> *Do we believe in anything, anymore?*
> *Say, that the doe is nuzzling her dead fawn,*
> *with a snort at stiffening, poisoned flesh.*

A man walking by a river finds a fossil like a conch, a horn.
He wants to offer it up in a glass case
but instead he lays it in my palm.

How do I sound this ancient stone?

> *Take my hand,*
> *in that dark*
> *when I face the mouth,*
> *my own mouth*
> *that only wants to chew,*
> *to feed,*
> *no matter what.*
> *Together we can render*
> *the silence*
> *of eighty deer*
> *plush and lost,*
> *that violation,*
> *the fury in this stone.*

New Prey

If I had a gun
and knew how
and it was the right season,
I could shoot her,
though I'd need five more
to make a meal,
they estimate.

Mourning dove,
you've been safe for five decades
until this one when the government
decides you don't deserve protection.

You're not a songbird. You're meat to eat.
You're a public nuisance with your gentle eye,
your gracing of stiff poles and sizzling electric lines.
Your grey flutter's an affront to efficiency.
Your eye is far too woeful for born-again politicians.
Even your name's an irritation.

We'll have no hint of grief.
We'll sight it unsuspecting,
slay it on cool mornings.
Eat its dead heart before night falls.

During War Times

This bright spring morning with the world so wounded,
the geese make a ragged victory over grey heads and skittish deer.
Maynard the dog doesn't know of war. I'm glad of that.
Though we all come in harm's way, here it's air so soft,
cottonwood trees so silver and dry-eyed to remind us
the world's gifts sometimes march unresisted to our center.

When will we surrender, be liberated into beauty
and sadness that must rise, in its salvaged colors,
like oceans of war dead reclaimed?

I walk down into the river valley today, the third day of this war.
Nine eagles come diving and delighting me, walking far below
with Maynard, who just wants to wander in the tall grass.

I hear dry stalk touching leaf, call of eagles mating, owl, duck.
I lie down on the rich layers of sedge, bark, water, soil
and listen to the earth sighing, waking ever. The little self slips away.

Just sun, oak tree, dog lapping water from a stream.
Nothing more real than praise and pleasure,
not the numbers of pounds of bombs,
not the heavy tread in the deserts of Iraq,
not even the air full of predictable
voices and pronouncements.

I close my eyes and imagine
all the generals, naked,
lying quietly with me in the tall grass,
lying without a sword,
all the senses on fire,
doing nothing to deserve this glory,
ours for the peaceful taking.

Certificate of Need

"The Minnesota Waste Management Board may certify need
for a repository for hazardous waste only if it has determined
there are no feasible and prudent alternatives."

What is feasible and prudent
when a trust is broken,
the atom split,
any cold war begun?

The earth is afraid of us.

When we have taken anyone
any way against her will or his,
it is prudent to come weeping
however we can weep,
with ideas or jokes
or what we are most, water.

And with many, many small
generosities in our hands.

And it is feasible that we lie
on the earth as if it were our body
and be mouth a moment
for one syllable of its pain.

Maybe even necessary.
Because the earth we all claim
we want to protect
is not filing her comments here.
She has no legal counsel

Continued

and doesn't understand
words like *negative impact*
and *intrinsic suitability*.

Only one word keeps appearing
on her certificate of need:

Listen.

Ghost Leg

You will need minds
stronger than steel,
wolf daughters, sons,
old ones, young,
to gnaw yourselves
free.

One limb
or wing of strength
to embrace
whatever it is that you love,
whatever will carry you
to that river that swallows
every loss.

Keen eyes,
instinct of the wild one
that however hunted
never stops
its flight to its beginnings.

The surest will,
deep as an ancient
river valley,
to imagine
whatever you need.

Whatever You Do

A Little Rapture

Soon the yellow finch will command like a cardinal,
a catbird strut with the industrious pheasant,
the red-tailed hawk kettle with the turkey buzzards,
a blue indigo bunting make a ruckus with the jay.

Soon you will realize feathers are music and meteors.
Soon, soon, you will feed only on delight
like the ruby-throated hummingbird,
like the great horned owl at night.

Then I will pick you three sprigs of river cedar
just flaunting her sea-green berries
and bring you prairie orchid
with her ivory-locked fragility.

I will set your cheek against purple blazing star
and let your hair stream with the prairie smoke.

You shall have the wind whisper over each inch of skin
and the tall bluestem grass to float in,
stepping just so lightly, so undaunted,
so safely across the new wilderness.

Witness

Close to the ground once,
she dwelled in snow drifts,
sang crystal cold,
learned in time
to spin blue orbs
from out green fingers.

The river rains fed her.
The earth chugged up her ragged limbs.
Stars stayed as far away as you
suppose you are from her.

She pledged herself to height,
flung her spires into brief
layers of sun and finches.

If eagles emerged,
they never landed there
where life was far too dense.

Her movement was all seasons.

Rich in witness,
rife with nature's luck,
her sap still runs
gold and heavy.

Trees I Have Known

They have an ease I envy.
They go with the wind,
crumble when it's time.

Once I made love inside
a huge hollowed out cottonwood.
Once I sat alone in a stunted oak,
waited till a doe stepped close.

When in despair, I touch a tree,
plant black stones around her base,
weave red ribbons into low branches.

I learn her body with my hands and eyes.

Trees give us beauty and breath,
try to draw us to them
on delicate lines
that could easily snap.

They promise that.

When I see an old stump
jagged and dark,
I lower my palms
to the fading rings,
rest them there.

We stand together
inside the widening circle.

Coming Back from That Time

The bones of some animal,
not large, I brought home.
Brought home the perfect rose cones
of the tamarack tree and blurred
photos of the yellow lady slippers
floating their buttery boats
near the flung bottle in the roadside ditch.

Brought back with me
memories of the women at the local bar,
beautiful in their own right, but
I think, my friends, we are not
beautiful as the tamarack.
We have to drag our sadness
everywhere, into our card games
and banter, into our smiling silences.

Come, let us walk out
in the dead of this June night
and wander in the swampy place,
carrying our lanterns of grief.

Let us brush against the wild larch
and melt in the glow of marsh marigolds
until we come to rest by bursting cattails
that stand like wrapped bodies
skewered, shedding every last softness.

At Last

This stays
when our feelings leave us empty
after every rage, every love that fails:

> Loon with her plaintive laugh,
> cottonwood tree, her thousand gentle hands,
> stars that soothe the scraped heart.

This stands
when our dwelling falls
and striations of fear bind us tight:

> Thicket rich in thorn,
> rugged beaver lodge,
> dark lairs and downy nests,
> one old tree to climb.

When our bodies blur like maple leaves
and our words commence to drown in dust,

> dreams gleam in the far swamp,
> desire tunnels under prairie roots,
> our last breath rides out on a stormy wind.

Whatever You Do

Whatever your race or age or color,
whoever we suppose you are,
you will not regret
those days you slipped away
from the sterile offices
or houses with their whirring demands,
even from wood to cut or corn to pound,
those days you walked upon the wild shore
or stood, looking up at the light
all splayed from the canopy of maple
and said nothing,
thought no thing
but how beauty flings itself
in our faces, knowing we need it
like water or air.

You will not regret
how you dared to speak
to a twisted tree,
went out to scatter prairie seeds
or let tears rain on some old stone.
You will not regret those hours and days
whatever forms they take.

No, at the end, you will hold them to you
with a strength that may surprise you.
Feeble perhaps, perhaps blind,
you will see everything then,
will hear the planets whirling
within you, peaceful chorus,
tumult of joy, tending you
like an ever faithful child.

No

She would not be clever.

She would be the tall grass
till it burned down, way down.

She would be red-tailed hawk
nailed to sky and ground.

She would not be wily
but be sedge at water's lips
and turn with a season
to brown dry web.

With the rocks she would
glisten dull, with oak
let go limb by gnarled limb.

She would not be wiser.
She would not be less.

At Sixty, Thinking How

When the father goes,
throwing his heart
like a worn-out engine valve,
the common loon comes
riding a cold lake,   .
seeding its laugh
in your soft pine arms.

When the mother leaves,
the brazen hawk scores wind
forty-four stories up
in downtown Chicago,
bequeathing territory, keenness,
a body of memory left
suspended above your shoulders.

But when your children
rush away to strangers' breasts
and break the tethers,
the kite lines to your sphere,
whole flocks are summoned,
grackles, finches, cardinals and crows,
to fly into your bed
and peck away your oldest need.

So, you will probably want to be with the birds at dusk
when the orchard oriole trills to serenade a dying sun
and the dauntless wren calls vociferous.
A tilted head, finally, blackbird's eye, then, mindless harmony.
No doubt you will want feathers, to have them in a row
or circling in a spendthrift way, sprouting wild nests in the staid trees.

Do the old birds' offspring fill their narrow beaks
or tuck them under flopping leaves?
Who registers their final notes?

Ah, no one needs to close those eyes where sky reigned each morning
or bless those bodies ragged and redeemed by storm and flight.

You will want to be with them.

To Those Preparing for Flight

What amber seed
      thought you?

Whose ochre bones
      fed you
and gleaming mouth
      sold your secrets to sun?

What violet rains
      slipped through your veins?

Which weather did you bow to,
      burgeoning green
            then dying into gold?

Does such resplendence make you ache?

And why so many of you
      to shatter all our simple sight?

Origins

Always we have been
brought forth by the trees
to be strung between bedrock and sky,
shaped for music,
surrendered to birds,
marked, worshipped,
folded back
into the wry forest's palm.

Always we are
for the climb, the strike,
the rot, the break of us,
permitting the breath
the ride earthward.

Our shames,
rings
the child traces.

Our stripped life,
home to every
lucid blessing.

When we understand
what the trees are.

Lightest of Rains

Slight upon two clinging dragonflies
still for a moment
on a grey lily pad.

Soft to the yellow-breasted bird
warbling alone
from his buckthorn.

Gentle over each human head
bent to peer
at water's edge.

Lightest of rains,
faintest
blessing.

Salve to the parched eye,
blithe for the young ones yet
simple enough for the roughest of skins.

Kisses to open the grasping hand,
silver to cool
the scalded brain.

Rivers of ease
for the old one's face
turning to stone.

Disperse

I love the sore prairie wind
that rides in March
and shakes the shorn wisteria,
fluffs the downy woodpecker's head,
makes us move to sheltered corners,
tie down our little stories.

That all might be airborne!

That love and wars
and all last words
might mount these breezes
and harmlessly disperse.

That the nine eagles
might enter then
to soar and summersault,
mate inside it all.

That we might love
the invisible
that finally whisks us
all away.

That Will Not Be Stilled

Far away someone stands near the stones birthed
before bison, before the massacres.

Lichen stars have written themselves on the stones.

The human body walks on the dried grass where the stones wait.

This is the beseeching, the prayer of ourselves,
the stones flooding like stars into the mind of night.

I listen to my heart.
I hear something beating out in the waves,
opening up like the throat of the oriole opens up spring green.

Trees are parting when that sound comes riding,
the only cave we came from, vibration that will not be stilled.

This is my singing
to the stone and earth, the river and tree and sky of us.

Birth comes hard and always this death inside it
which is why the new day.

Disappear

The perfect day—
when trees and prairie
grass and sky
enter you,
empty of rage
or sadness.

Fallen bark
lies with you
like a faithful
old husband.

Your hands,
shards of ice,
break apart,
melt.

Your hair
begins to flower
ahead of the season.

The perfect moment
comes when you
can't get up.

You are held
steady
as an eagle's
pinfeather, light
as lark's
memory.

You are
perfectly
gone.

About the Author

Florence Chard Dacey is the author of three other poetry collections: *The Swoon, The Necklace,* and *Maynard Went this Way.* She is a recipient of a Loft-McKnight Poetry Award. Through school and community residencies and workshops, she teaches creative writing to people of all ages. She has lived in Cottonwood, Minnesota for forty years and has long been active in peace, environmental, and social justice issues. Her website is www.florencedacey.com.

Author photo by Joland Mohr.

About the Artist

Elizabeth Erickson, longtime friend of the writer, Painter, Professor at the Minneapolis College of Art and Design, has a commitment to dreams coming true.

Artist photo by Kate Zehren

Printed in the United States
145371LV00001B/1/P